Nelson
Handwriting

Pupil Book A

D1354269

Nelson

Handwriting patterns

Look at these patterns.

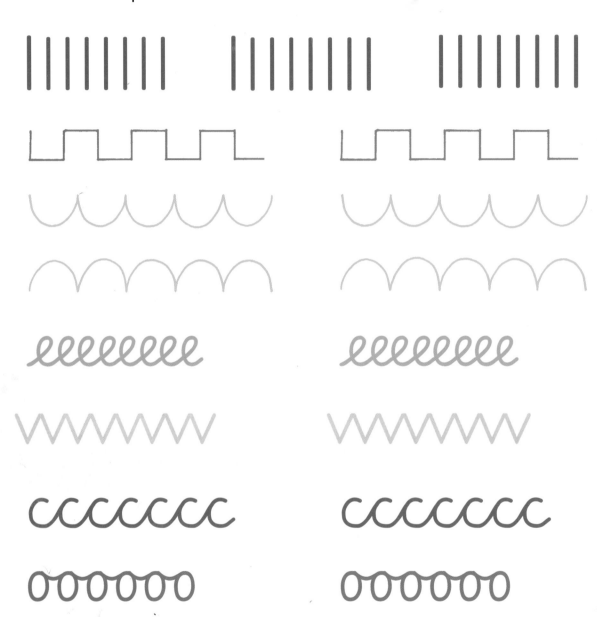

Copy the patterns.
They will help you with your handwriting.
Hold your pencil lightly.
Let the tip of your pencil flow over the paper.

Have fun with the patterns.
Here are some ideas to try.

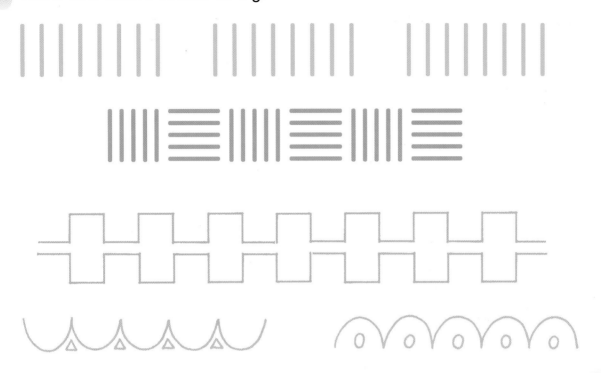

Try drawing the patterns in different sizes and colours.

3

Look at these groups of letters.
Each group is formed in a different way.

litjkuy   vwxz

mrnbph   esf

cadoqg

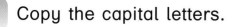 Copy the letters.

Look at these capital letters.

ABCDEFGHIJK

LMNOPQRS

TUVWXYZ

Copy the capital letters.

4

Now look at these numerals.

0 1 2 3 4 5 6 7 8 9

Copy the numerals.

Look at these groups of letters.
Ordinary letters

a c e i m n o

r s u v w x z

Letters with ascenders (tall letters)
These are much taller than ordinary letters.
t is not as tall as b, d, f, h, k and l.

b d f h k l t

Letters with descenders (letters with tails)
These are much deeper than ordinary letters.

g j p q y

Copy each group of letters.

Look at these two pictures.
What differences can you see?

Look at these two pieces of writing.
What differences can you see?

A quick brown fox
jumps over the lazy dog.

A quick brown fox
jumps over the lazy dog.

In this book you will be learning to do joined-up writing.
You need to learn two new letter shapes.

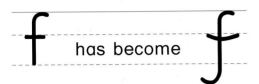

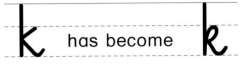

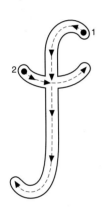

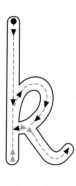

Trace these letters several times with your finger.
Get the feel of them.

Practise these letters until you can write them easily and well.

ƒ ƒ ƒ ƒ ƒ ƒ ƒ ƒ ƒ ƒ

k k k k k k k k k k

in name and

The first join is used when we join any letter in **Set 1** to any letter in **Set 2**. Look carefully at these joins.

Set 1 letters

a c d e h i k l m n s t u

Set 2 letters

a c d e g i j m n o p
q r s u v w x y

Trace this pair of letters several times with your finger.
Get the feel of the first join.

The first join is made from the end of one
letter to the beginning of the next.

$i + n \longrightarrow in$

The join is like the upswing of the
swings pattern.

Copy these patterns and joined words.

ᴜᴜᴜ ᴜᴜᴜ ᴜᴜᴜ ᴜᴜᴜ

ᴜᴜᴜ ᴜᴜᴜ ᴜᴜᴜ ᴜᴜᴜ

ᴜᴜᴜ ᴜᴜᴜ ᴜᴜᴜ ᴜᴜᴜ

in in in in

in in in in

in in in in

Look at these ip words.
They have been made with the first join.

d → ip	dip dip dip
h → ip	hip hip hip
l → ip	lip lip lip
n → ip	nip nip nip
t → ip	tip tip tip

Copy the words in the box.

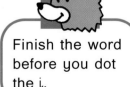

Finish the word before you dot the i.

Write the words.

d → im *dim*

h → id _____

t → in _____

d → in _____

d → id _____

h → im _____

l → id _____

In all the words you make, all the letters should be joined.

Look at these *um* words.
They have been made with the first join.

hum   mum

Copy the *um* words.

Copy these patterns.
They will help you with the first join.

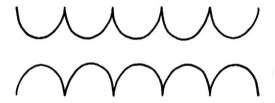

> Don't lift your pencil between the beginning and ending of *hum* and *mum*.

Copy what the children are saying.

 mmmmm

 yum yum yum

 yummy yummy

Copy these words.

mug tug hug dug

Copy these sentences.

A bug can hug.

A bug can tug.

A bug can jump in
a mug.

dine ten deed

This is how **Set I** letters join to e.

Join lots of es like this:

eeeeeee   eeeeeee   eeeeee

Now copy these pairs of letters.

ae ce de ee he ie ke
le me ne se te ue

Copy these words.

hen men ten
ten men and a hen

Copy these words.

Underline the letter that comes before the *e* in each word.

bake

bite

dance

hide

tie

sleep

mend

Look at these *ay* words.
They have been made with the first join.

day hay lay may

Copy the *ay* words.

Sam has written a diary.
Copy what she has written.

On Sunday I
played all day.

Copy these patterns.
They will help you with the first join.

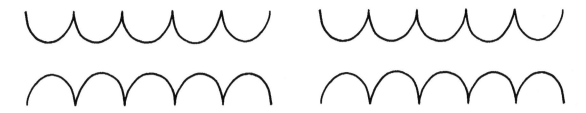

Copy these pairs of letters and words.

ar ar ar ar ar ar

car tar jar bar

Copy this sentence.

We can go far in a car.

How are you
getting on?
Look at the checklist.
Keep practising!

The letter s can be joined to any **Set 2** letter with the first join.

Look at these pairs of letters.

sa sc se si sm sn

so sp sq su sw sy

Copy the pairs of letters above.

Copy these words.

sing snap spin sad

When the letter s comes **after** a join from a **Set I** letter, it changes its shape.

pans lids names

Look carefully at the shape of the s. What do you notice?

Copy the words above.

Copy these pairs of letters.

as ds es is ks ls ms ns

Copy these, and write the missing words.

one pen   six pens

one pan   six _____

one lid   six _____

one cat   six _____

cub lick tell

The second join is used when we join any letter in **Set I** to any letter in **Set 3**. The join meets the ascender about halfway up. You continue the join to the top of the ascender and then come down again.

Set I letters	Set 3 letters
a c d e h i k →	b f h k l t
l m n s t u	

Trace this group of letters several times with your finger. Get the feel of the second join.

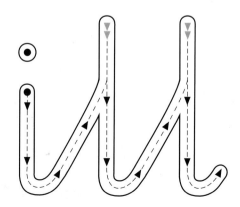

Copy this pattern.
It will help you with the second join.

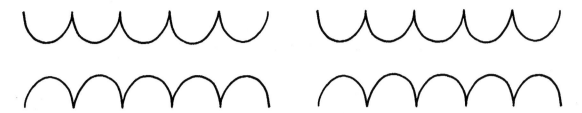

Copy these groups of letters.

ill ill ill ill ill

Copy this sentence.

Jack and Jill went up the hill.

We use the second join to join c to k.
Look at these *ack* words.

back hack lack
pack packet
jack jacket

Copy the *ack* words.
Now copy this sentence.

Jack has a sack
on his back.

Take care how
you join c to k.

Copy this pattern.
It will help you with the second join.

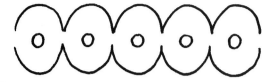

Copy these groups of letters.

ick ick ick

Finish each group
of letters before
you dot the i.

Copy these words.

pick kick tick lick

Now copy these.

You tick it.

You lick it.

You kick it.

You pick it.

We use the second join to join c to h,
and to join s to h.

ch ch ch ch

sh sh sh sh

Take care how you
join c or s to h.

Copy the pairs of letters above.

Now copy these words.

chap chat chip chin
chick chill check

she shed shell sheep
ship shy shack shin

Choose *ch* or *sh* to complete each word.
Write the words.

chimp   __ip   __ick

__ed   __at   __eep

__in   __ell

How are you
getting on?
Look at the checklist.
Keep practising!

We use the second join to join any letter in **Set I** to t.

at et it lt nt ut ct

⬤ Copy the pairs of letters above.

Remember that t is not as tall as the other letters with ascenders.

⬤ Copy these words.

bat cat hat mat sat

⬤ The words in this sentence are in the wrong order.
Write the sentence carefully.

sat hat. The on cat the

Don't forget the capital letter and the full stop!

Practice with f

We use the second join to join any letter in **Set I** to f.

af   ef   if   lf   uf

Copy the pairs of letters above.

Now copy these.

What if the sun suddenly went blue?

What if a giant came after you?

toy want hard

The third join is used when we join any letter in **Set 4** to any letter in **Set 2**.

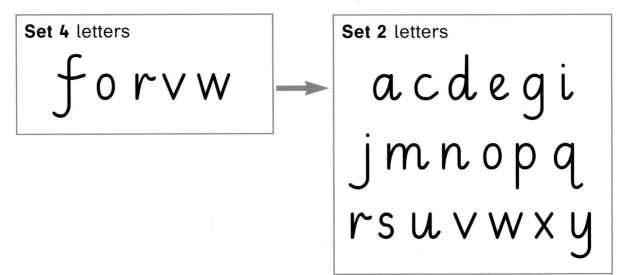

Set 4 letters		Set 2 letters
f o r v w	→	a c d e g i j m n o p q r s u v w x y

Trace this pair of letters several times with your finger. Get the feel of the third join.

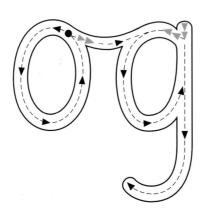

When you are using the third join, keep the letters well spaced.

28

Copy these pairs of letters.

og og og og og og

Copy these words.

dog frog cog

Copy these sentences.
Use one of the words above to fill the gap in each sentence.

A ____ is in a fog.

A ____ is on a log.

We use the third join to join f or r to any letter in **Set 2**.

fa fi fo fu

ra ri ro ru

○ Copy the pairs of letters above.

○ Copy these words.

fan   run

found   ran

fig   round

fun   rig

○ Join the words that rhyme.

30

We use the third join to join v or w to any letter in **Set 2**.

va vi vo vu

wa wi wo wu

Copy the pairs of letters above.

Take extra care with
the joins from v and w.

Now copy these.

a worm in a wig

a vole in a vase

a wasp on a wall

a van on a volcano

ae When we join a **Set 1** letter to e, we use the first join.

we When we join a **Set 4** letter to e, we use the third join.

What difference can you see between the two ways of joining to e?

Copy these pairs of letters, using the third join.

we   we   we   we   we

Copy these words.
Underline the we join in each word.

Take care how you join w to e.

<u>we</u>ak web wed

went wept were well

Copy these pairs of letters.

fe fe fe fe   oe oe oe oe

re re re re   ve ve ve ve

Copy these words.

cave wave   toe doe

fire tired   wife knife

re fe ve oe

Use one of these pairs of letters to finish each word.
Write the words.

Take extra care with the joins from f and r.

kni__   fi__

t__   ca__

us   When we join a **Set 1** letter to s, we use the first join.

ws   When we join a **Set 4** letter to s, we use the third join.

What difference can you see between the two ways of joining to s?

Copy these pairs of letters, using the third join.

ws   ws   ws   ws   ws   ws   ws

Copy these words.
Underline the ws join in each word.

bo<u>ws</u>   rows   mows

crows grows slows blows

Now copy these.

rows of bows

rows of crows

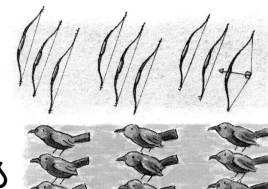

Copy these patterns.

ccccccccc ccccccccc
ccccccccc ccccccccc

Copy these pairs of letters.

rs rs rs rs rs rs rs rs rs

os os os os os os os os os

vs vs vs vs vs vs vs vs vs

Now copy these.

two cars

three bars

four jars

five stars

How are you
getting on?
Look at the checklist.
Keep practising!

smoke girl rob

The fourth join is used when we join any letter in **Set 4** to any letter in **Set 3**.

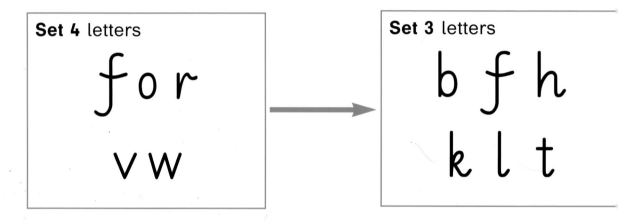

Set 4 letters	Set 3 letters
f o r	*b f h*
v w	*k l t*

Trace this pair of letters several times with your finger. Get the feel of the fourth join.

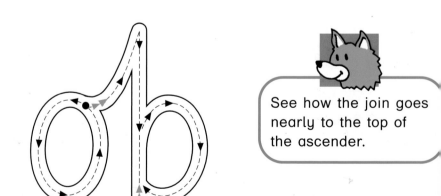

See how the join goes nearly to the top of the ascender.

Copy these pairs of letters.

ob   ob   ob   ob   ob

Copy these words.

cob   hob   lob   mob   job

Copy these sentences.

I am Bob. I am a robber.

My job makes me sob.

The fourth join – Practice with fl

We use the fourth join to join f to l.

fl fl fl fl fl fl

Copy the pairs of letters above.

Copy these words.

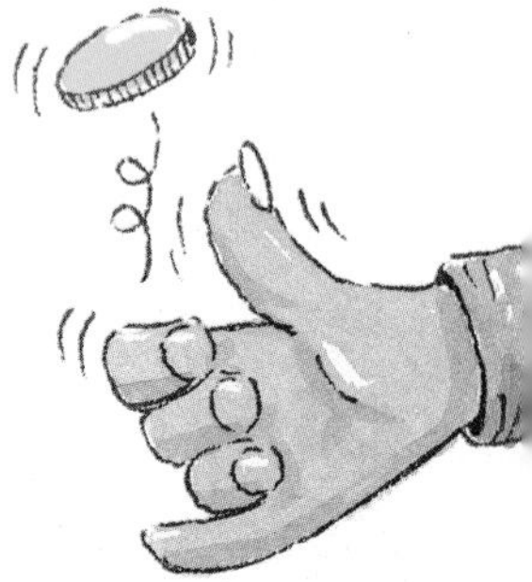

flat flap flack

flit flip flick

float flop flock

flapjack

flipflops

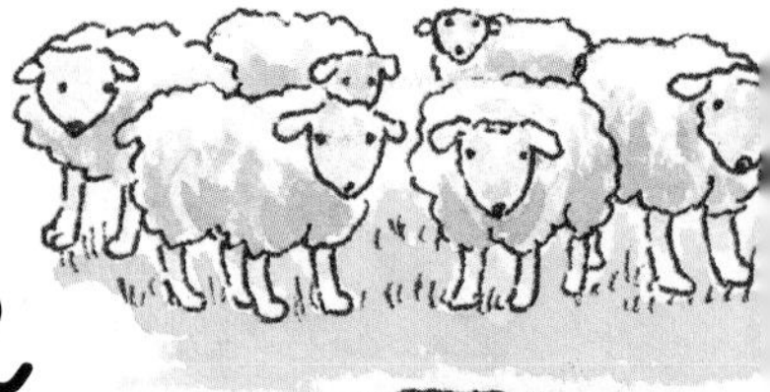

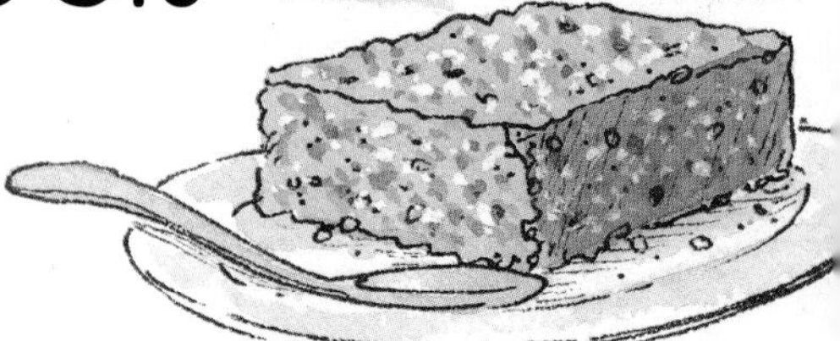

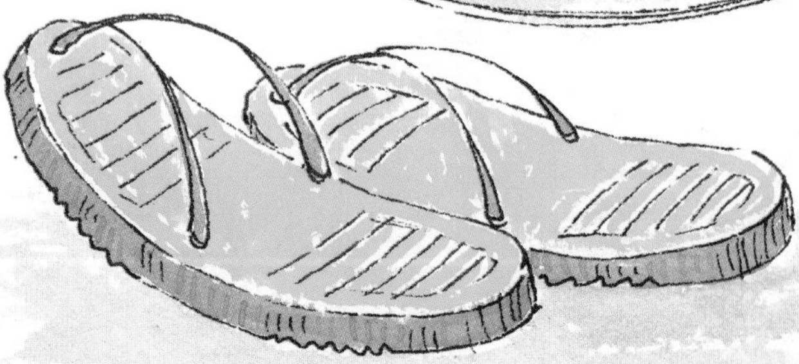

We use the fourth join to join r to k.

rk rk rk rk rk rk

○ Copy the pairs of letters above.

○ Copy these words.

park bark dark mark

○ Copy these sentences.
Fill each gap with one of the words above.

A dog can _____.

At night it is _____.

Mum will _____ the car.

My pen makes a _____.

We never make a join after any of these
eight letters.

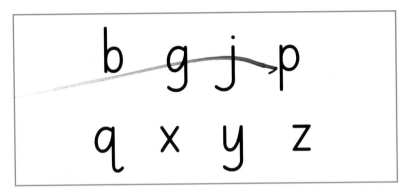

Never make a
join **to or from** z.

Copy these words.

big   bigger   biggest

happy happier happiest

boxes yo-yo got opened
queen lizard

Copy these sentences.
Use one of the words above to fill each gap.

The queen ___ out of bed.
She _____ the ____.
The _____ found a
yellow ____ and a
lazy ____.

Look at the capital letters on page 4.
A capital letter is never joined to another letter.

Write all the capital letters three times.
Write these children's names in alphabetical order.

Carra   Adam   Dan

Ben   Emma   Grace

Khayyam   Indira   Harry

Jake   Lucy   Freya

 Mark

 Olivia

 Always use a capital letter to begin someone's name.

 Nadeem

 Raza

 Quentin

 Petra

 Una

 Sam

 William

 Zak

 Tasneem

 Vaheem

 Youssef

 Xerxes

Copy these patterns.

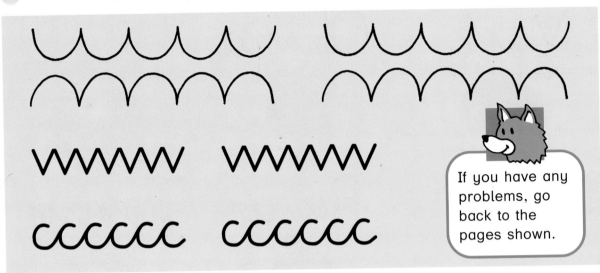

If you have any problems, go back to the pages shown.

Copy these pairs of letters and words.

The first join (pages 8 – 19)

mi ac ce ds

mice ace dance adds

The second join (pages 20 – 27)

ck al ib sh

lick call bib ship

The third join (pages 28 – 35)

rm fe ws va

farm fence cows van

The fourth join (pages 36 – 39)

rl ot ft rk

girl hot left ark

Now copy this sentence.
All the letters of the alphabet are in it.

The five boxing lizards jump quickly into the water.

Copy this poem in your best handwriting.

Our family

We laugh and cry,

We work and play,

We help each other

Every day.

The world's a lovely

Place to be,

Because we are

A family.

by Mary Ann Hoberman

Copy this party invitation in your best handwriting.

4 High Street

To Katy

Please come to my

birthday party

at 4 o'clock on

Saturday, April 7th.

From Ben

How well have you done?
Look at the checklist.

Copy these patterns carefully.

⌣⌣⌣⌣⌣ eeeeeee

ccccc oooooo

You have come to the end of Pupil Book A. This is a good time to check your writing.

Copy these words in your best handwriting.

sun limp cap mend

chick tells shine mate

stars found went wife

rob flock girl off

Copy this sentence in your best handwriting.

A quick brown fox jumps

over the lazy dog.